EFFECTIV
FOR BUSINESS,
AND PERSONAL USE

A GUIDE TO SUCCESSFUL CORRESPONDENCE

Publishing Since 1978

NEAL PUBLICATIONS, INC.
127 WEST INDIANA AVENUE
P. O. BOX 451
PERRYSBURG, OHIO 43552-0451, U.S.A.

Publishers of:

"Effective Phrases for Performance Appraisals"
A Guide to Successful Evaluations

"Effective Resume Writing"
A Guide to Successful Employment

"Your Slice of the Melon"
A Guide to Greater job Success

EFFECTIVE LETTERS
FOR BUSINESS, PROFESSIONAL AND PERSONAL USE

A GUIDE TO SUCCESSFUL CORRESPONDENCE

Neal Publications, Inc.
127 West Indiana Avenue
P. O. Box 451
Perrysburg, Ohio 43552-0451   U.S.A.

First Edition	1989
Second Printing	1990
Third Printing	1991
Second Edition	1994
Second Printing	1995
Third Printing	1997
Third Edition	1999

Printed in the United States of America

ISBN 1-882423-14-3
SAN 240-8198
Library of Congress Catalog Card Number: 98-91432

FOREWORD

This practical book is designed for the busy person who needs general purpose letters covering a broad range of subjects. Most of the model letters have been time proven in actual use.

The best letters are short and simple. They are positive and convey warmth and friendliness.

It is suggested that you personalize the letters to the greatest possible degree.

EFFECTIVE LETTERS FOR
BUSINESS, PROFESSIONAL AND
PERSONAL USE

CONTENTS

6

I

ELEMENTS OF AN EFFECTIVE LETTER

Numerous books are available on the subject of letter writing. Many of the letter writing books contain virtually identical information.

What you really need to know about writing an effective letter can be reduced to the following:

1. Keep it short.
2. Use short words and paragraphs.
3. Avoid archaic phrases.
4. Keep the tone pleasant and active.
5. Use "you" and "your" rather than "I" and "we" as much as possible.
6. Be friendly and courteous.
7. Apply the time proven criteria of what, when, where, why, how and who?
8. Inspire action.
9. Use correct spelling and punctuation.
10. Print the letter on high quality paper.
11. Use a quality envelope.

You can improve the effectiveness of your letters by reviewing copies of previous correspondence.

Place yourself in the position of the receiver. Do your letters incorporate the points listed on the previous page? With practice and a determined effort, letter writing can be fast, easy and effective.

II

MODEL LETTERS

Dear (   ):

I wish to express my sincere appreciation to (organization) for being named (award) of the year.

This award would not have been possible without the support of (name).

I shall continue to provide the (quality of teaching — finest product, etc.) which has made this worthy recognition possible.

Thanks again for this fine honor.

Dear (   ):

In anticipation of even a more productive and prosperous future, I accept this (award) as (top salesperson — best nurse, etc.).

Our fine organization, splendid management and strong support programs have all made my dreams possible.

I wish to thank you for this tribute and I pledge that I will continue to do my utmost for the good of (organization).

ACCEPTANCE
— Award

Dear (   ):

I would like to thank the (organization) for the (award). I accept it with pride and satisfaction. It is with great pleasure that I work for (organization).

This coveted honor would not have been possible without the guiding help of (name).

Thank you again for this cherished award. I look forward to the future with renewed dedication and enthusiasm.

———————

Dear (   ):

Words cannot express my feelings upon receiving the (name) award.

With deepest appreciation, I accept this honor and hope that I can live up to the high expectations of our great organization.

I could not have achieved this recognition alone. (Names) have helped me along the path to reach our mutual goals.

Thank you for your support and for this fine honor

ACCEPTANCE
— Employment Offer

Dear (   ):

    I wish to thank you and (   ) for giving me the opportunity to join the (   ) organization. I am very pleased to accept the position of (   ) in your (   ) Department. The position offers the exact opportunity which I have been seeking. I know that I will be a valuable addition to your firm.

    As discussed, I will begin on (   ) with a starting salary of ($). In the meantime, I will complete all the employment forms and obtain the physical examination.

    I really enjoyed my interview with you and (   ). I am looking forward to starting this career with great enthusiasm.

_____

ACCEPTANCE
— Employment Offer

Dear (   ):

I am pleased to accept the (description) position offered in your letter of (date). The position offers a fine opportunity.

Your confidence in me is greatly appreciated and I am eager to apply my education, skills and enthusiasm.

I am looking forward to the beginning of a long and successful career.

———————

Dear (   ):

It is a real thrill to receive your employment offer for the position of (   ) in your (   ) Department.

I am pleased to accept the position. It is my understanding that the starting salary will be ($) monthly with a possible year-end bonus.

As requested, I will immediately contact (name) to receive additional information.

I certainly appreciate this opportunity and look forward to making a strong contribution to (name of organization).

ACKNOWLEDGEMENT
— Customer Complaint

Dear (   ):

Thank you for your letter concerning our associate (name).

It is certainly disturbing to receive such a letter. I am immediately asking our (title of superior) to investigate the situation.

I appreciate your advising me of this incident and you may be assured that it will have my personal attention.

———————

Dear (   ):

Thank you very much for writing to me about your dissatisfaction with the handling of your (   ).

In order that you may receive prompt service, I am sending your letter to the personal attention of (name), Regional Manager. You will hear from (Mr., Mrs., Ms.) (name) within a few days. Meanwhile, I have requested that a full report be sent to me.

Thank you again for writing to me, (Mr., Mrs., Ms. [name]) and giving us an opportunity to look into this for you.

ACKNOWLEDGEMENT
— Damaged Merchandise

Dear (   ):

Thank you for returning the (   ) which you recently purchased from us.

Despite our efforts to meet the highest standards of quality control, we occasionally ship merchandise which inadvertently escapes the attention of our inspectors. Obviously, this situation occurred with your (   ).

In checking the serial number, we find that your (   ) was produced on a day when we incurred several power failures due to a major storm. As a result, the plating process was inferior.

We are today shipping a replacement to you by next day air. We are also making arrangements to pick up your (   ) which will be thoroughly examined.

We are sorry for the problem and hope you will continue to be a valued customer.

———————

ACKNOWLEDGEMENT
— Employee Compliment

Dear (   ):

I wish to thank you for your letter of (date) regarding our representative (name).

In this day and age, it is seldom that people will take the time to write a letter commending individuals. On the other hand, if they seem to have any kind of complaint, it is generally expressed promptly and quite clearly.

I sincerely appreciate your taking the time to make these fine comments and I will personally convey them to (name).

———————

ACKNOWLEDGEMENT
— Employee Compliment

Dear (   ):

Thank you very much for your letter complimenting our (name of employee).

It is always a pleasure to receive such a letter. Your comments encourage all (name of company) employees to provide the finest possible service.

Too often, outstanding performances by employees goes unnoticed. We greatly appreciate customers who take the time to let us know of their complimentary remarks

Thanks again and best wishes.

ACKNOWLEDGEMENT
— Letter

Dear (   ):

Thank you for your letter of (date).

(Mr., Mrs., Ms.) (name) is currently out of the office and will return on (date).

You may be assured that your letter will receive prompt attention next week.

ACKNOWLEDGEMENT
— Lost Shipment

Dear (   ):

Thank you for advising us that you never received the (quantity) of (item) covered on your purchase order no. (   ) dated (   ).

The (item) was shipped on (date) by (carrier). A tracer is being initiated and we will notify you as soon as information becomes available.

If we are unable to determine the status, we will immediately release a duplicate shipment.

We are sorry for the problem and assure you of our prompt attention.

———————

ACKNOWLEDGEMENT
— New Account

Dear (   ):

It is a real pleasure to enclose a signed copy of our marketer's agreement. We trust this agreement will represent the beginning of a long and mutually profitable business relationship.

You will be glad to know that our entire organization is enthusiastically developing plans to support your sales efforts. I cannot help but feel extremely confident of our ability to achieve outstanding success.

(Name), our (position), will be contacting you regularly. If you need any further assistance, please do not hesitate to let me know.

———————

Dear (   ):

Thank you for your letter concerning the retail price of our product.

(Name of Company) does not establish retail prices. We provide marketers with suggested resale prices. Marketers are free to set their own prices.

We consider our (product) to be of very high quality and encourage retailers to sell on the basis of value rather than price.

We trust you will understand our position and hope you will continue to be a valued user of our products.

ACKNOWLEDGEMENT
— Request to Distribute Products

Dear (   ):

Thank you for your letter of (date).

New distribution in your area is the responsibility of our (Mr., Mrs., Ms.) (name), (title).

I am immediately forwarding your request to (Mr., Mrs., Ms.) (name), who will soon contact you.

Your interest in marketing our product is greatly appreciated.

—————————

ANNOUNCEMENT
— Employee Promotion

Dear (   ):

We are pleased to announce that (name) has been promoted to (title). The appointment is effective (date).

(He/She) is well qualified for the position having served most recently as (title).

All requests for (description of services) are to be directed to (first name).

We know you will extend the fullest cooperation to (him/her).

———————

ANNOUNCEMENT
— Holiday Closing

Dear (   ):

This is to inform you that our manufacturing facilities and offices will be closed on the following holidays:

HOLIDAY   MONTH   DAY   YEAR

These closings will enable our employees to observe the holidays with their families.

As always, fax transmissions and computerized order entries will continue to be accepted on a 24 hour basis.

———————

ANNOUNCEMENT
— New Employee

Dear (   ):

We wish to inform you that (name), our representative, has left the employ of our Company to pursue other interests.

Please welcome our new representative (name), who will soon be calling on you. (Name) has a wealth of credentials in our industry. (He/She) is a graduate of (   ) and has a solid background in (   ).

You will find (name) to be very knowledgeable and helpful. (He/She) is looking forward to working with you.

We are proud to have (first name) represent us and I know you will also think highly of (him/her).

———————

ANNOUNCEMENT
— New Employee

Dear (   ):

  We are pleased to announce the appointment of (name) to the newly created position of (title).

  (Name) is a recent graduate of (school) where (he/she) majored in (subject). (He/She) worked two summers for us as an intern in the (name) Department and is very knowledgeable of our policies and programs.

  (Name) will gladly assist you in your (order processing — inquiries, etc.).

———————

ANNOUNCEMENT
— New Plant

Dear (   ):

We are extremely pleased to announce the completion of our new manufacturing facility in (city, state).

The (size) square foot plant features the most advanced manufacturing equipment to provide the highest quality (product). Ample capacity is now available to supply our growing customer needs.

If you are visiting the (city) area, we would be pleased to arrange a tour of the new facility. Tours may be scheduled by contacting our Public Relations Department one day in advance of your visit.

May we take this opportunity to thank you for your continued business.

APOLOGY
— Invoice Previously Paid

Dear (   ):

    Thank you for your letter advising us that our invoice no. (   ) was previously paid.

    You are absolutely correct! Our overdue notice dated (   ) was sent in error. We have already implemented measures to avoid a reoccurrence.

    We regret this mistake and hope you will continue to be a valued customer.

———————

APOLOGY
— Product Complaint

Dear (   ):

I have just learned that you are not satisfied with your recent purchase of (   ).

Our Mr. (   ), Service Representative will soon contact you to resolve the problem.

If the situation is not completely settled to your satisfaction, please call me.

We are sorry for the problem and any inconvenience it may have caused.

———————

APOLOGY
— Quality Problem

Dear (   ):

It is disturbing to learn of the problems that you are encountering with our (name of product).

Our representative, (name) will meet with you on Wednesday morning, April (   ) to investigate the problem. (He/She) will obtain samples which will immediately be forwarded to our Quality Control Department for analysis.

We have today shipped by overnight freight (quantity) (product). (Company name) stands 100% behind our products and this situation will be promptly resolved to your satisfaction.

We regret the inconvenience and assure you of our fullest cooperation.

———————

APPLICATION
— Membership

Dear (   ):

I wish to apply for membership in the (name). The enclosed forms have been completed to the best of my ability.

After discussing my application with (name) and (name) who have recommended me, I know that I will be an active and supportive member.

I am looking forward to a favorable reply.

_____

APPRECIATION
— Business Anniversary

Dear (   ):

As we begin to celebrate our tenth anniversary, I wish to thank you for your continued business.

Over the past ten years, we have made every effort to provide the best of products at a fair price. Now, we are looking forward to our next ten years and assure you that our commitment to excellence will continue.

In appreciation for being such a good customer, we believe you deserve something special. Our representative will soon be calling on you and personally deliver an anniversary gift. I am sure you will enjoy it.

Thanks again for your loyal support which has contributed so much to our mutual success.

———————

APPRECIATION
— College Visit

Dear (   ):

I wish to thank you for the many courtesies extended to me during my visit on (date).

I was very impressed with your strong academic programs. The tour of the campus was a most enjoyable experience.

After spending a day on your campus, I am convinced that (school) is my first choice of universities. I will soon forward a completed application form.

Thank you again for a very pleasant and rewarding day.

APPRECIATION
— Complimentary Remarks

Dear (   ):

Thank you for the kind words that were said about me at the (dinner — meeting, etc.).

It is people like you who make this job very rewarding.

APPRECIATION
— Gift, General

Dear (   ):

   (Name) and I wish to thank you for the beautiful (gift).

   I am sure it will provide us with many hours of happiness.

   Thanks again and we are looking forward to seeing you.

APPRECIATION
— Gift, General

Dear (   ):

   Thank you for the beautiful (gift).

   When I use it, I will always think of your (generosity — kindness — thoughtfulness — friendship).

   You are a true friend!

APPRECIATION
— Gift, Graduation

Dear (   ):

Thank you for the graduation gift.

I appreciate your remembering me at this exciting time in my life.

I like the (gift) very much and will think of you often.

APPRECIATION
— Gift, Holiday

Dear (   ):

Thank you so much for the (gift). (Name) and I used them a number of times over the holidays.

Our thanks to you and (name).

We hope the New Year is good to both of you.

APPRECIATION
— Gift, Wedding

Dear (   ):

   The beautiful (gift) you chose as our wedding gift is cherished.

   (Date) was the happiest day in our lives. (Spouse) and I were so glad you could be here to share our joy.

   Thank you for the gift and your friendship.

———————

Dear (   ):

   We love the beautiful (gift) which you sent us for our wedding. Thank you so much for your kindness and thoughtfulness.

   We hope you will visit us soon in our new home.

———————

Dear (   ):

   It was so nice of you to remember us on our wedding day with such a lovely gift. The (gift) is perfect for our home.

   We were sorry that you were not with us but hope that you will visit us soon.

Dear (   ):

(First name) and I were disappointed that you could not share the joy of our wedding day. We know that you were with us in spirit.

We will certainly enjoy using the (gift) that you sent us.

Thank you so much for your thoughtfulness.

———————

Dear (   ):

The lovely (gift) that you sent us is greatly appreciated. We enjoy using it everyday.

(First name) and I were so happy that you could be with us on our most joyous day.

Thank you for your kindness and friendship.

———————

APPRECIATION
— Gift, Wedding

Dear (   ):

The memories of our wedding day were enhanced by your presence.

Thank you for your thoughtful gift. When we use the (gift), we will always think of you.

Your friendship means a lot to (spouse) and me.

APPRECIATION
— Handling of Complaint

Dear (   ):

Many thanks for your letter of (   ).

My claim has been happily concluded and you have reaffirmed my confidence in the high standards of (company name).

It is most gratifying to receive your letter and I certainly appreciate your fine assistance.

Dear (   ):

I wish to express appreciation for the many courtesies extended to me during my recent visit.

I was most impressed with both your outstanding facilities and the talents of your personnel.

As a result of our discussions, I am confident that my background and experience would be a valuable addition to your staff. I would welcome an opportunity to contribute to the continuing success of your company.

Thank you again, and I look forward to hearing favorably from you.

———————

Dear (   ):

I wish to thank you for the interview on (date).

I was very impressed with your fine people and facilities.

Your current opening for a (position) continues to be of great interest to me. I am confident that my education, experience and enthusiasm will enable me to excel in this position.

I hope to hear favorably from you.

APPRECIATION
— Interview

Dear (   ):

I would like to thank you for the opportunity of visiting you on (date) and talking with (name)

I feel that my education, talents and goals are congruent with the constructive and forward looking plans of (organization). I know I can do a good job for you and wish to be seriously considered for the position of (title).

Your consideration of my qualifications would be greatly appreciated.

I look forward to hearing from you.

———————

APPRECIATION
— Loan Payment

Dear (   ):

We wish to express our appreciation for your payment in full of (loan — mortgage — account, etc.).

Your fine payment record reflects personal integrity and responsibility.

You will always be welcomed as a valued customer.

We are looking forward to the opportunity of serving you again.

———————

APPRECIATION
— Personal Favor

Dear (   ):

I would like to express my appreciation for allowing me to use your (condominium — house — apartment, etc.).

It was just delightful being able to stay in such comfort. Your generosity and friendship will long be remembered and cherished.

Thank you again for your kindness.

———————

APPRECIATION
— Personal Favor

Dear (   ):

Many thanks for allowing my wife and I to use your boat during our recent vacation. We especially enjoyed the beautiful sunsets while on the water.

In appreciation, we left a small gift in your storage locker. We know you will enjoy it!

Thanks again and best wishes.

———————

APPRECIATION
— Product Testimonial

Dear (   ):

Thank you very much for your kind letter complimenting the quality of our (product).

It is always gratifying to receive such a letter because your comments indicate that our commitment to achieving the highest quality standards is successful.

You may be assured of our continuing efforts to provide the superior quality and performance that have made (brand name) (number 1 — a leader) in the marketplace.

Your taking the time to write us is greatly appreciated.

————

Dear (   ):

I wish to extend my sincere appreciation for (your or department's) fine efforts in rescuing the gentleman from the (   ) bridge on (   ).

Your exemplary performance is a splendid tribute to your professionalism and dedication to duty. The success of this rescue would not have been possible without your important contribution.

I am sure that the entire community joins me in expressing appreciation for your outstanding accomplishment.

APPRECIATION
—Publicity

Dear (   ):

I wish to express my appreciation for the splendid article on our Company which appeared in your (date) issue.

The article was excellent in every respect and I hope that your readers enjoyed it.

Thanks again for your fine coverage.

APPRECIATION
— Quality Rating

Dear (   ):

Thank you for your letter of (date).

We certainly appreciate receiving the certificate in recognition of (Company's) superior quality rating.

Innovative product planning and the attainment of manufacturing excellence are a corporate commitment of the highest priority.

You may be assured of our continuing dedication to achieving outstanding quality and performance.

APPRECIATION
— Referral of
Prospective Customer

Dear (   ):

I just want to thank you for referral of (name).

Personal recommendations are very important to our business and I greatly appreciate your thoughtfulness.

APPRECIATION
— Religious Service

Dear (   ):

Thank you for the service of (marriage – burial) for (name).

It meant so much to me to hear such (joyous – inspirational – comforting – thoughtful) words.

At this (happy – sad) time, when friends and family are gathered together, we appreciate and give thanks for our faith.

I will long remember your many kindnesses to me and my family. Thank you again for all you have done for us.

———————

Dear (   ):

I wish to thank you for the many courtesies extended to me during my call of last week.

It was a real thrill to tour your new facility and you have every reason to be proud of it.

With regard to your spring promotion, this will confirm that we will ship (no.   ) (item) at a price of ($) per (quantity) with payment terms of (   ) F.O.B. (   ). Shipment is scheduled for (   ).

We certainly appreciate your order and assure you of our fullest support.

———————

APPRECIATION
— Speaker

Dear (   ):

On behalf of the (organization), I wish to thank you for your fine speech at our (date) meeting.

Our members thoroughly enjoyed your talk along with the most interesting discussion. I am sure that our membership now has a better understanding of (describe).

Thank you again for your excellent presentation.

———————

Dear (   ):

On behalf of (organization), we wish to express our appreciation for your support of the (event).

The success of this event would not have been possible without our valued sponsors.

Thank you again and we hope you share our good feelings in knowing that your contribution helped to provide (benefits).

———————

APPRECIATION
— Teacher

Dear (   ):

(Spouse's name) and I would like to thank you for all you have done for (name of child) during this school year.

Your patience and kindness are greatly appreciated. (Name of child)'s attitude toward schools has improved greatly under your knowledge and guidance.

Thanks again.

———————

Dear (   ):

Please accept our thanks and appreciation for all the kindness you have shown (name of child) this year.

Through your efforts, (name of child) has been motivated and endeavored to do (his/her) best work.

———————

APPRECIATION
— Year-End Bonus

Dear (   ):

As the end of the year fast approaches, I wish to express my sincere appreciation for your fine efforts.

Our success in (year) would not have been possible without your important contribution.

We are looking forward to (next year) with much confidence. Our (products – programs – promotions, etc.) will be strengthened in all areas and we intend to fully capitalize on our growing opportunities.

In recognition of your fine performance, I am enclosing a bonus check for ($).

Congratulations again and best wishes for continued success.

———————

BUDGET
— Excessive Variance

Dear (   ):

A review of your department expenditures through the third quarter indicates that your total variances exceed your budgeted amount by almost 7%.

It is essential that you take prompt measures to ensure that your expenditures for the year end are within budget.

Please give this situation your immediate attention.

———————

BUDGET
— Projection Request

Dear (   ):

Enclosed is your (time period) budget projection form.

The first column lists all expenditure categories for the current year. Column two shows the budget for each category. The third column lists the variances through the third quarter.

Enter your projected expenditures for the coming year in the space provided. You may add, delete or revise categories as needed. Management has requested that your projected budget expenditures are not to exceed 2% over the prior year.

Budgeting is one of your most important responsibilities and warrants your close attention and best efforts.

Please return your completed projection by (   ). A budget review discussion will be scheduled at a future date.

———————

CANCELLATION
— Business Function

Dear (   ):

Due to unforeseen circumstances, we find it necessary to cancel our scheduled convention for (month), (day), through (day).

In accordance with our agreement, we are giving you (no.) days advance notice.

We regret the need for this cancellation and hope to use your fine facility at a future date.

———————

Dear (   ):

Confirming our phone conversation of today, please consider this our damage claim under policy no. (   ).

On (   ), at approximately (   ), a strong wind blew a number of shingles off a portion of our roof. Enclosed are photographs of the damage.

We will appreciate your prompt inspection of the damage and issuing a repair authorization.

Thank you.

———————

CLAIM
— Lost Shipment

Dear (   ):

On (   ), we shipped via (carrier) one carton of (   ) to the following address:

> Mr. and Mrs. John Doe
> 1234 Any Street
> Your State and Zip

The tracking number is (   ) and the insured amount is ($).

Since you have been unable to locate the shipment, we are herewith enclosing our receipts covering the missing items in the amount of ($).

Your prompt cooperation in forwarding a check for ($) including shipping charges will be appreciated.

———————

Dear (   ):

Business involves obligations between two parties.

The obligation of (Company name) was fulfilled when your order was shipped. Enclosed are copies of your purchase order no. (   ), proof of delivery and our invoice no. (   ) dated (   ) for ($).

Your obligation is to pay the full amount owed.

Immediate payment is required.

———————

COLLECTION
— Past Due

Dear (   ):

    Your payment of our enclosed copy invoice no.
(   ) dated (   ) for ($) is past due.

    Perhaps you have misplaced the invoice or there is another reason for your failure to pay.

    We hope you will give us the courtesy of a prompt reply.

————————

COLLECTION
— Second Notice

CERTIFIED MAIL
RETURN RECEIPT REQUESTED

Dear (   ):

Despite our previous notice, we have not received payment covering your invoice no. (   ) dated (date) for ($).

Your payment is now (no.) days overdue.

If you have encountered any problems with the order, please advise us. Enclosed is proof of delivery.

Please forward immediate payment to avoid more stringent measures.

———————

COLLECTION
— Third Notice

Dear (   ):

Your payment of our enclosed copy invoice (no.) dated (date) for ($) is seriously past due.

We are planning to place your account with a collection agency on (date) unless we receive your payment.

If you will immediately forward payment, your credit rating will not be jeopardized.

Immediate payment is required.

———————

COMPLAINT
— Company Representative

Dear (   ):

    We are sorry to inform you that, in our opinion, your employee (name) was (discourteous — rude — arrogant — belligerent — unclean) on the evening of (date) at (time).

    Specifically, your employee (describe the incident).

    In accordance with your policy of being a caring company, we believe you would want to know about this unfortunate situation.

    We felt it was important to inform you so that you can take corrective action and maintain your excellent reputation.

—————

COMPLAINT
— Customer Follow-Up

Dear (   ):

The enclosed copy letter from a (   ) and our reply are self-explanatory.

Please call on (   ) at the earliest opportunity and arrange to resolve the problem. If necessary, you have approval to replace the damaged inventory with new stock at no cost.

I will appreciate receiving a report of your call by (   ).

Dear (   ):

After using the (product) for (a period of time), we found it to be defective as follows:

1.
2.
3.

According to the warranty, we are entitled to a refund or replacement. The (product) is being returned today by (method of shipment) to your service center located at (address). A copy of our receipt is enclosed with the shipment.

Please forward a full refund including the cost of shipping which is indicated on the receipt.

We appreciate the good name and reputation of your company and know that you will comply with our wishes as soon as possible.

———————

Dear (   ):

The enclosed (product) which we purchased from you on (date) is (defective — does not operate properly, etc.).

A copy of our receipt and guarantee is also enclosed.

Please forward a replacement as soon as possible.

COMPLAINT
— Product

Dear (   ):

On (date), I purchased a new vehicle from your dealership.

Within ten days after taking delivery, we noticed a significant miss in the engine. On (date), we took the car back to your dealership and your (name), Service Manager, advised us that the problem was corrected. After driving about two miles, we again noticed the problem. Once again, we took the car back. We were again advised that the problem was repaired.

Enclosed are copies of five service repair forms describing the identical problem which continues to this day.

At this point, we wish to receive another vehicle. If we do not receive a replacement vehicle, we plan to contact the state Attorney General's office and initiate legal proceedings under the Consumer Protection Lemon Act.

I hope that we can rely on the fine reputation of your firm to provide us with a new vehicle. I will call on you on (   ) at (   ) to discuss our request.

COMPLAINT
— Request For Credit

Dear (   ):

    This is to inform you that during the month of
(   ), we experienced four days without cable
service. The outage was reported at (   ) on
(   ).

    Since we pay a monthly charge ($)
amounting to a daily charge of ($), please
issue a credit for ($).

    Thank you for your cooperation.

———————

COMPLAINT
— Service

Dear (   ):

As a long time customer of (name of company), I am writing to express dissatisfaction with the service at the store located at (address).

The store operates in the evenings with only three cashiers. As a result, long lines occur virtually every evening.

Many customers become disgruntled while waiting and this situation does not reflect the progressive policies of your fine company. I am sure that many customers shop elsewhere in order to avoid the waiting.

I would appreciate your looking into the situation and taking corrective action.

———————

Dear (   ):

This is to inform you that we have not been satisfied with the recent lawn mowing at (street) in (city).

Two tenants have complained about the high grass. They report that the crew is merely skimming the grass and it needs mowing two or three days later.

If the mowing does not improve, we have no alternative other than to hire another service.

Please make every effort to immediately cut the grass shorter.

_____

CONFIRMATION
— Meeting Arrangements

Dear (   ):

This will confirm our telephone conversation of today concerning our forthcoming meeting.

We will require a suitable room to accommodate (no.) persons on (day of week), (month), (date).

The room set-up is to be (no.) round tables seating (no.) persons each. In addition, we will require a podium with a public address system along with a screen to be at least (feet) by (feet) in size.

We will bring our own projection equipment, but will require a projection stand.

The meeting will begin at (time) with coffee breaks to be scheduled for (time) and (time). Coffee, tea, juice and rolls are to be available for the (time) break. Coffee, tea, juice, iced tea and soft drinks are to be available at the (time) break. Ice water is to be on each table throughout the day.

Lunch is to be served in a separate room between (time) and (time). We have selected luncheon menu no. (   ).

As stated in your letter of (date), the cost of the meeting room, coffee breaks, and lunch will be ($). It is our understanding that our total cost including the (— %) tax will be ($).

(Continued)

I will be in charge of the arrangements and will be assisted by (name).

We are looking forward to a very successful meeting. If you have any questions, please feel free to contact me at any time.

CONGRATULATION
— Accomplishment

Dear (   ):

The entire (department — school, etc.) joins me in congratulating you for (describe).

We are so proud of your achievement and know it was only possible through your dedication and perseverance.

———————

Dear (   ):

Congratulations on exceeding your (month) sales quota.

It is this type of winning performance that continues to keep (Company) (number 1 — a leader, etc.).

Again, congratulations on your outstanding accomplishment, and keep up the good work.

———————

CONGRATULATION
— Award

Dear (   ):

For outstanding achievement in business — medicine, etc.) the (name) award is given to (name) on behalf of your many friends and associates. Through your many years of devoted effort you have consistently and conscientiously contributed to the betterment of all segments of this (industry — hospital, etc.).

This award is made in recognition of (describe) and as a tribute to your exemplary performance as a truly progressive and farsighted (business person — librarian, etc.).

Congratulations and best wishes.

———————

Dear (   ):

Congratulations on receiving the (year and name) award.

You have certainly earned this most deserving recognition.

Our entire organization is proud of your professional achievement and we extend best wishes for continued success.

———————

77

CONGRATULATION
— Business Anniversary

Dear (   ):

The 50th anniversary of (organization) is a significant occasion marking your many years of dedicated service to (your customer — the industry, etc.).

(Organization) congratulates you and extends our best wishes for continued success.

––––––––––

Dear (   ):

On behalf of our entire organization, I wish to congratulate you on the (no. of years) anniversary of your company.

Your many years of success is a fine tribute to your outstanding products, service and business policies.

Congratulations and best wishes for another (no. of years) of progress.

––––––––––

CONGRATULATION
— Business Anniversary

Dear (   ):

As we begin to celebrate our (no. of years) anniversary, I wish to thank you for your continued business.

Over the past (no. of years), we have made every effort to provide the best of products at a fair price. Now, we are looking forward to our next (no. of years) and assure you that our commitment to excellence will continue.

In appreciation for being such a good customer, we believe you deserve something special. Our representative will soon be calling on you and personally present an anniversary gift. I am sure you will enjoy it.

Thanks again for your loyal support which has contributed so much to our mutual success.

———————

CONGRATULATION
— Promotion

Dear (   ):

Congratulations on your promotion to (title).

I can think of no one who is better qualified for this position.

Again, congratulations and best wishes for continued success.

———————

Dear (   ):

Please add my name to the many well wishers who have offered you congratulations on your promotion.

I wish you all the success you deserve in your new position.

———————

Dear (   ):

I wish to extend warmest congratulations on your promotion to (title).

Your solid experience and many years of dedicated service will surely contribute to your continued success.

Again, congratulations and best wishes.

CONGRATULATION
— Promotion

Dear (   ):

I was extremely pleased to learn of your promotion to (position). It is always a pleasure to see a deserving friend rewarded for (his/her) efforts and hard work.

Your management has selected a real performer with outstanding qualifications.

You have my best wishes for health, happiness and success in your new position.

_____

CONGRATULATION
— Retirement

Dear (   ):

Congratulations on your retirement.

Your many years of dedicated service have certainly contributed to the success of (organization).

You are going to be missed by all your friends and associates. We hope you will continue to keep us informed of your activities.

Best wishes to you and (spouse) for a long and happy retirement filled with good health and much happiness.

———————

Dear (   ):

What a happy time this must be for you. The (school — group, etc.) wishes you and your family all the best that life can bring.

Congratulations on your retirement and best wishes for the future.

———————

CONGRATULATION
— Retirement

Dear (   ):

With best wishes and congratulations on your retirement, (the company — school, etc.) would like to present you with this (gift).

No one deserves this honor more than you. Your many years of devoted service have touched us all.

We wish you good luck, good health and many years of happy retirement.

Dear (   ):

With sincere gratitude for the many years of devoted service, the (company — hospital, etc.) wishes you a happy and healthy retirement.

Your many friends and associates will miss you. However, we are glad that you now have the opportunity to do some of the things you have long planned without the responsibilities that you have shouldered.

You have been a very valued employee and will always be welcomed at the (company — library, etc.).

CONGRATULATION
— Retirement

Dear (   ):

    We are so happy to join you in a special time of happiness and reward for your many years as a loyal employee.

    Although no one will ever "fill your shoes," your willingness to share knowledge and ideas will long be remembered in our organization.

    We sincerely hope you find retirement to be enjoyable and we wish you life's best.

—————

CONGRATULATION
— Retirement

Dear (   ):

I wish to express my personal gratitude for your many years of loyal service to (organization). Although you worked only several years in my department, I soon became aware of your outstanding qualifications and dedicated performance.

The ties and binds of nearly (no.) years are not easily broken and we will surely miss your enthusiasm and commitment to excellence. Your service has endeared you to many members of the (company — organization).

I hope you will enjoy many years of happy and healthful retirement. My sincere thanks and best wishes to you and (spouse).

———————

CONGRESSIONAL MEMBER
— Special Request

Dear (   ):

I am writing to request your help in solving a local problem.

As a result of federal budget reductions, the U.S. Weather Bureau no longer maintains service at (name) Airport after 11:00 p.m.

My Company operates three aircraft specializing in air freight. Our major customers are automotive assembly plants located within fifty miles of the airport. Most of our flying is required at night.

With winter fast approaching, we are extremely concerned about the safety of night flying. The absence of local weather reports may require us to cancel many flights which would have a very serious impact on our business.

I would greatly appreciate your efforts to reinstate night weather service at (name) Airport. I am looking forward to hearing from you.

CONGRESSIONAL MEMBER
— Urging Action

Dear (   ):

I am writing to support passage of Senate Bill (no.).

As a (small businessman — farmer — retiree, etc.). I feel that (government aid — reduced government aid, etc.) will (harm — hurt, jeopardize) the (market — environment — industry, etc.). The impact would be (disastrous—devastating, dangerous) to my (customers — members — health, etc.).

Senate Bill (no.) would resolve the situation by (describe). It will provide a (freedom of choice — more funds — reduced taxes, etc.) to thousands of Americans.

For these reasons, I urge you to work for and support passage of Senate Bill (no.).

I would be interested in receiving your views on this bill.

_____

CRITICISM
— Expense Report

Dear (   ):

Your expense report for the week ending (date), included two customer dinners amounting to a total of ($). Wine charges alone were ($).

This expenditure for (no.) persons is unacceptable and reflects poor judgement on your part.

It is the responsibility of every employee to ensure sound cost control.

We expect you to conform to our expense policy guidelines in the future.

Please be guided accordingly.

———————

Dear (   ):

An open line of communications is vital for a continuing beneficial relationship between your firm and (Company name). As your company is one of our most valued customers, we wish to make certain that you are completely satisfied with our products.

Please take a few minutes to complete and return the enclosed survey form. Information gathered from the form will be forwarded to the appropriate department head for review and action.

We welcome constructive criticism and comments so that we may make continuous improvements.

Your business is greatly appreciated and we hope to serve your needs for many years to come.

CUSTOMER GOODWILL
— Publicity

Dear (   ):

I thought you would be interested in the enclosed article on your company which appeared in our local newspaper.

It is always a pleasure to learn of the strong sales increases of one of our most valued and longtime customers.

I hope that our (product) helped to contribute to your outstanding success.

————————

DONATION
— Acknowledgement

Dear (   ):

This will acknowledge your request for a donation to the (organization).

We are forwarding your request to our Contributions Committee and you will be notified of a decision on approximately (date).

You may be assured that your request will be given every consideration.

DONATION
— Refusal

Dear (   ):

Thank you for your letter of (date).

The policy of (Company) is to contribute to charitable organizations only in the communities where we maintain manufacturing operations.

Accordingly, we are unable to contribute to (organization).

We wish you every success in your efforts for this most worthy cause.

DONATION
— Refusal

Dear (   ):

Thank you for your letter of (   ) requesting a donation to your organization.

Our Board of Directors has established rigid guidelines for all company donations. Unfortunately, your organization does not meet our requirements with respect to the areas served.

Although we are unable to contribute, we wish you every success with your campaign.

———————————

DONATION
— Refusal

Dear (   ):

Thank you for your letter of (   ) requesting a donation to the (   ).

Unfortunately, we are not in a position to make
a contribution at this time. We receive numerous
requests for donations and give careful consideration to each organization.

If you will forward a year end financial report
of your organization, we will be glad to review your
request at a future date.

Your interest is appreciated.

DONATION
— Transmittal

Dear (   ):

    We are very pleased to enclose a check for ($) as a donation to the (   ) Clinic.

    Our Board of Directors has designated that these monies are to be used for medical research in the field of cancer. I have been authorized to contact you with the request that you direct these funds to a research project that shows much promise.

    We are glad to make these funds available to such a worthy cause and hope they will make a major contribution to your nationally acclaimed research programs.

———————

Dear (   ):

    In recognition of the splendid efforts of (organization), we are pleased to again make a donation. Enclosed is our check (no.) for ($).

    We are proud that our Company can make this generous contribution for such a worthy cause.

    Keep up the good work!

Dear (   ):

    In recognition of the fine efforts of your organization, we are pleased to again make a donation. Enclosed is our check (no.) for ($).

    We are looking forward to your continuing strong programs in support of (medical research — truth in advertising, etc.).

FAREWELL
— Employee Departure

Dear (   ):

You have heard that I have accepted a new assignment to head up the (office location) for the (Company). Briefly, the job will entail (describe). It is a most interesting challenge.

My replacement as (title) is (name). (First name) possesses a wealth of knowledge and has an excellent understanding of our (Company) programs and philosophy.

I wish to express my thanks and appreciation for our association and your cooperation over the years. I hope and trust your future will be blessed with good health and filled with much happiness.

My very best to you and your family.

———————

Dear (   ):

(Company name) wishes to thank our valued suppliers for their support and cooperation during the past year.

As the Holiday Season approaches, we wish to remind our vendors of our long-standing policy which prohibits our employees from accepting any gifts or gratuities. This policy ensures and preserves the integrity of our business relationship.

Your cooperation in adhering to our gift policy will be appreciated.

May we take this opportunity to extend best wishes to you and your employees for a Happy Holiday Season.

———————

GIFT POLICY
— Business

Dear (   ):

As the Holiday Season approaches, we wish to thank our valued suppliers for their excellent service and support.

We believe this is also an appropriate time to remind our vendors that (name of company) has a long-standing policy of prohibiting employees from accepting or giving gratuities of gifts, etc.

Your cooperation in refraining from gift giving will ensure the continued integrity of our business relationship.

May we take this opportunity to extend best wishes to you and your employees for a Prosperous and Happy New Year.

———————

Dear (   ):

During the Holiday Season, we take great pleasure to express our appreciation for your continued business.

Valued customers like you are the foundation of our success.

May your Holiday Season be filled with joy and the coming year bring all good blessings to you and your associates.

———————

HOLIDAY GREETING
— Business

Dear (   ):

During the year, in our fast paced world, we often overlook the important friendships that are the foundation of true business relationships.

One of the great pleasures of the Holiday Season is the opportunity to extend cordial greetings to those whose friendship we value so highly.

It is in this spirit that we thank you for your business and express sincere appreciation for the pleasant association we enjoy with you.

May you have a bright and Prosperous New Year filled with all good blessings.

———————

Dear (   ):

We wish to express our warmest appreciation for the business you have given us during the past year.

It is most gratifying to value you as a customer and a good friend. In the days ahead, we promise our earnest efforts to deserve your continued patronage.

At this Holiday Season, we send our best wishes and hope that peace, health and prosperity will be with you.

———————

Dear (   ):

As another year draws to a close, I wish to express our sincere appreciation for your business. We enjoyed a very strong sales increase in (year) which would not have been possible without valued customers like you.

For (year), we will be announcing (new products —campaigns, etc.). We are excited about these plans and are eager to share them with you.

Thanks again and best wishes for a bright New Year filled with all good blessings.

Dear (   ):

As the end of the year fast approaches, I wish to express my sincere appreciation for your business.

Our success would not be possible without the valued support of customers like you.

For (year), we will strive to earn your continued trust and confidence.

Our entire organization joins me in extending best wishes for a Prosperous New Year.

HOLIDAY GREETING
— Business

Dear (   ):

As another year draws to a close, we wish to express our appreciation for your valued business.

Satisfied customers are the true basis of our success. In this respect, we are committed to providing the type of quality products and service that will ensure your continued trust and loyalty.

May you and your associates enjoy the merriest of Holiday Seasons and the New Year bring you many good fortunes and all rich blessings.

———————

Dear (   ):

Sometimes we do not understand why sickness and suffering come into our lives. However, we all know that the power of prayer will sustain us through these difficult times.

Our thoughts and prayers are with you during this time of need.

———————

Dear (   ):

Please know that all of us at (organization) are wishing you a speedy recovery from your recent (illness — operation).

The place doesn't seem the same without you.

Get well soon.

———————

Dear (   ):

We were so happy to hear that your surgery was successful.

You have our best wishes for a speedy recovery.

———————

ILLNESS

Dear (   ):

I have just learned that you have been under the weather and wish to extend best wishes.

If you will follow your doctor's orders, I am sure that you will be back on your feet in no time.

Best wishes for a speedy and complete recovery.

––––––––––

Dear (   ):

During this time of (sickness — illness), we realize the importance of family and friends.

We want you to know that all your friends at (organization) are (pulling for — cheering for) your recovery.

––––––––––

Dear (   ):

We have just learned of your recent (illness — surgery).

Please know that our thoughts and (prayers — concerns) are with you at this time.

––––––––––

INTRODUCTION
— Employment Referral

Dear (   ):

This letter is to introduce (name) to you. (First name) has worked (no.) years for us.

I can tell you first hand that (he/she) has excellent experience and has completed (special training, etc.) with the utmost capacity for transferring knowledge to practical application.

We believe that (name) deserves consideration by your (firm — school, etc.) for the position of (title).

It is a pleasure to highly recommend (him/her).

———————

INTRODUCTION
— Promoted Employee

Dear (   ):

    We are pleased to announce the promotion of (name) to the position of (title) covering your (area — account).

    (Name) joined (Company) in (year) and has steadily risen through our organization. (He/she) has a thorough knowledge of our products and is well qualified to assist you.

    We will appreciate you extending a warm welcome to (first name).

―――――――

INVITATION
— General

Dear (   ):

    You and (spouse — a friend) are cordially invited to attend a (dinner — banquet, etc.) (in honor of —   to celebrate) (describe). The (dinner — banquet, etc.) will be held on (month, day, date) at (location). Cocktails will begin at (p.m.) with dinner at (p.m.).

We are looking forward to seeing you.

R.S.V.P.

INVITATION
—Meeting

Dear (   ):

    Please plan to attend a meeting of department managers on (day, month, date) at (time) in (location).

The following subjects will be discussed:

    1.
    2.
    3.

    If you are unable to attend, please send a representative.

INVITATION
— Meeting

Dear (   ):

A Division Managers' meeting will be held in (city and state), (month, day, date).

Please plan to arrive on the evening of (day, date) at the (Name) Hotel located at (address). You have been preregistered.

Attached is a complete agenda. In particular, please be prepared to discuss (subject).

The meeting will conclude at (   ) on (month, day, date). We suggest that you schedule all flight departures after (   ) local time.

We are looking forward to a very productive meeting.

———————

INVITATION
— Private Sale

Dear (   ):

   In appreciation for your continued business, we are pleased to enclose two invitations to our upcoming private sale. The sale will be held at our main store located in the (   ) Shopping Center.

   The invitations will allow you to purchase any item in the store at 15% off. Some items will be offered at 20% off the marked price.

   This is our way of saying thanks for your past patronage.

   We look forward to seeing you at this special sale for special customers.

———

INVITATION
— Speaker

Dear (   ):

As Program Chairman of the (city) chapter of the (organization), I am inviting you to speak at our meeting on (day, month, date).

The meeting will be held at the (name) Hotel located at (address). Dinner will be served at (time) prior to the meeting.

As you may know, our organization is dedicated to advancing the field of (marketing — nursing, etc.). Your outstanding accomplishments on behalf of (marketing — nursing, etc.) are well known to our members and they are eager to meet you.

We will pay all expenses including lodging and transportation from your home.

I hope you will be able to address our group. We look forward to hearing from you.

———————

INVITATION
— Speaker

Dear (   ):

I am the Chairman of the Program Committee for the (organization). Would you consider speaking to our group at (time) on (date)?

Although our group is small, we do have some funds available for guest speakers. Please send us any information concerning your fees, equipment needed, etc.

Thank you for your consideration. We look forward to hearing from you.

———————

PRICE INCREASE
— Announcement

Dear (   ):

Despite our continuing efforts to control costs, we have found it necessary to announce a price increase effective (date).

The new prices will apply to all orders shipped after (date). Attached is a new price schedule with suggested retail prices.

We will continue to provide you with the quality of products and service you have come to expect.

Our representative will soon be contacting you to review the new prices and discuss the powerful marketing programs that will support your (year) sales goals.

———————

PRODUCT CHANGE
— Discontinuance, Obsolescence and Replacement

Dear (   ):

Effective (month), (day), (year), product no. (   ) will be discontinued and considered obsolete.

Item no. (   ) will replace and supersede item no. (   ). The new Item offers the following product improvements.

1.

2.

3.

Item no. (   ) is assigned to price category no. (   ) and stocking category no. (   ). Enclosed are several new catalog pages. Additional pages may be obtained from our representative.

All recommendations previously specifying the superseded number will be covered by the new item. Returns of type no. (   ) will be accepted through (month), (day), (year).

The new (product) reflects our continuing dedication to providing outstanding product superiority.

———————

PURCHASE ORDER
— Appreciation, Large Order

Dear (   ):

I just want you to know that we greatly appreciate your large order which we received today.

We shall continue to do our very best to earn your confidence

Thanks again.

———————

Dear (   ):

I wish to thank you for the large order which we received today.

We will continue to provide the high quality product and service that have earned your trust and confidence.

Thanks again.

———————

PURCHASE ORDER
— Appreciation, Routine Order

Dear (   ):

Thank you for your order.

We hope you are fully satisfied with your (item).

Your purchase is greatly appreciated and we look forward to your continued business.

Dear (   ):

Thank you very much for your recent order.

We hope you will be pleased with the merchandise.

Your purchase is greatly appreciated and we look forward to again supplying your needs.

PURCHASE ORDER
— Check or Credit Card Number Missing

Dear (   ):

Thank you for your order. Unfortunately, we are unable to ship the requested item because you failed to enclose a check or credit card number.

If you will return the enclosed order form with a method of payment, we will be happy to ship immediately. You may also call or fax us with a credit card number.

Your interest in our products is greatly appreciated and we look forward to receiving your order.

———————

PURCHASE ORDER
— Check Received Without Order

Dear (   ):

   Thank you for your check (no.), for ($)
which we are herewith returning.

   We have been unable to determine the reason
for this check. If you wish to place an order, please
refer to the enclosed catalog. If you will specify an
item and return a check or provide us with a credit
card number, we will be pleased to ship immediately.

   Your interest is greatly appreciated and we look
forward to receiving your order.

_____

PURCHASE ORDER
— Order Delay

Dear (   ):

Thank you very much for your order covering (quantity of product).

Demand for this item has exceeded our highest expectations. As a result, we are temporarily out of stock.

Our manufacturing group is giving the highest priority to producing this item. Availability is planned for (date) and your order is scheduled to be shipped on (date).

We are sorry for the delay and any inconvenience it may have caused.

Dear (   ):

Thank you for your order no. (   ) dated (   ) for (   ).

Due to an overwhelming demand for this/these item(s), we are temporarily out of stock.

Our plant is working overtime to replenish inventories. Your order will be given priority handling with shipment scheduled for (   ).

Your cooperation and understanding will be greatly appreciated.

PURCHASE ORDER
— Placement Of

Dear (   ):

Please consider this our purchase order for (quantity) model no. (   ) (product) size (   ) in (   ) color. The purchase order number is (   ).

We understand the cost will be ($) each F.O.B. (   ) with payment terms of (   ).

Please ship by motor freight and bill as follows:

SHIP TO: _____

_____

_____

BILL TO: _____

_____

_____

All invoices, packing slips and correspondence must include the purchase order number. If shipment cannot be made by (   ), please notify us.

We are looking forward to receiving the merchandise.

_____

PURCHASE ORDER
— Rescheduling

Dear (   ):

This is to inform you that we have found it necessary to reschedule shipment on your purchase order no. (   ) due to circumstances beyond our control.

The recent (hurricane — tornado — flood) destroyed the section of the container plant that produces the bottles needed to meet your reguirements. Our supplier has assured us that every measure is being taken to promptly resume production.

Your order is now scheduled to be shipped on (   ).

We regret any problem this delay may have caused and trust you will understand the situation.

———————

Dear (   ):

This is to inform you that all purchases by (Company name) must be authorized by our Purchasing Department.

Our purchase order number must appear on all shipping documents, packing lists, invoices and correspondence. Partial shipments must also be clearly indicated on all documents.

Invoices for goods or services that have not been properly approved or are lacking the required information will be returned to the vendor unpaid.

We place a high value on good relationships with our suppliers. (Company name) expects to receive the best possible goods and services that will keep us competitive in the marketplace. In return, you will be extended every courtesy and opportunity to supply our needs.

With your cooperation, we look forward to your continuation as a valued supplier.

_____

RECOMMENDATION
— Business Project

Dear (   ):

 As you know, sales of the (product) line have declined for the past two years. I have given considerable thought to measures that will increase (product) sales.

 Enclosed is a marketing research study conducted in selected markets. The most significant finding is that dealers are stocking competitive (product) because our packaging does not lend itself to perforated fiberboard display.

 In view of this study, I propose that we initiate a market test offering our best selling (product) in new packaging designed for perforated fiberboards. We estimate that the total cost of the study including prototype packaging and test advertising would be ($).

 If successful, we would estimate a (   )% increase in (product) sales amounting to an additional gross profit of ($).

 I recommend that we conduct a six month test as described above. May I have your approval to proceed?

_____

RECOMMENDATION
— Character

Dear (   ):

I have known (name) for over (no.) years. (He/She) is a (neighbor — former employee, etc.) who enjoys an excellent reputation in the community.

(First name) is a person of the highest character and integrity. (He/She) is a responsible and trustworthy person.

It is a pleasure to offer comments on this fine individual.

If you require any additional information, please do not hesitate to contact me.

———————

RECOMMENDATION
— Club Membership

Dear (   ):

It is my pleasure to recommend (name) for membership in the (club).

I have known (name) for more than (no.) years and have been associated with (him/her) in business for the same length of time. I am sure that (he/she) and (his/her) family would uphold the high traditions of (club).

I fully recommend that you act favorably on (his/her) application.

RECOMMENDATION
— Employment

Dear (   ):

(Name) was employed as a secretary in the (sales — advertising, etc.) Department of (organization) during the period (date) through (date).

(His/Her) job performance was outstanding in every respect. The quantity and quality of (his/her) work was consistently high and (name) displayed accuracy, thoroughness and initiative in carrying out all assignments. (He/She) possesses excellent word processing skills.

(Name) worked harmoniously and effectively with others and was an important contributor to the success of the department.

It is a pleasure to recommend (name) for a secretarial position. (He/She) would be a very valuable addition to any organization.

―――――――――

RECOMMENDATION
— Employment

Dear (   ):

(Name) (attended — worked) for the (organization) during the period of (date) through (date).

In the time that I have known (name), (his/her) work has always been of the highest quality. (He/She) excels in (describe).

It is a pleasure to recommend (name) for a position with your (hospital — library, etc.).

RECOMMENDATION
— Personal

Dear (   ):

In response to your request, I have known (name) for (no.) years.

(He/She) was a close neighbor for (number) years. (Name) is exceptionally competent. (He/She) is well educated, highly motivated and displays strong leadership qualities.

I am pleased to highly recommend this fine person.

REFUSAL
— Employment Application

Dear (   ):

Thank you for forwarding your resume.

Unfortunately, we do not have any openings which are suitable for your qualifications and interests.

Your resume will be kept on file for ninety days. If any appropriate opportunities arise, we will contact you.

Your interest in our firm is certainly appreciated and we wish you every success.

———————

REFUSAL
— Employment Inquiry

Dear (   ):

Thank you for your letter inquiring about employment opportunities with (organization).

Unfortunately, we have no available positions which would appropriately match your background and qualifications.

We suggest that you direct your inquiry to the industry placement services offered by the following associations:

1.

2.

3.

Your interest is appreciated and we extend best wishes for every success in achieving your employment objectives.

———————

Dear (   ):

Thank you for your letter of (date).

We appreciate and value your opinion. However, our policy has always been to (describe). Consequently, we are unable to (describe).

We believe our position is reasonable and we hope you will continue to (purchase our product — patronize our stores, etc.).

_____

Dear (   ):

Thank you for your letter of (date).

Our policy is (describe).

We trust you will understand our position and we hope to have the opportunity of serving you again.

_____

REFUSAL
— Inferior or Damaged Product

Dear (   ):

This is to inform you that our order no. (   ) was received today.

Initial inspection has revealed many damaged (items). Enclosed are (no.) samples of unsalable (item).

Please have your representative contact us to review the shipment and make an adjustment.

By a copy of this letter, we are informing your Accounts Receivable Department that payment will be delayed pending settlement of the problem.

———————

REFUSAL
— Information on Former Employee

Dear (   ):

    This will acknowledge receipt of your request for personal information concerning (name), our former employee.

    Our firm does not release information on former employees other than the fact that (name) was employed by us from (   ) to (   ) in the position of (   ).

REFUSAL
— Payment

Dear (   ):

    We have received your invoice (no.) dated
(   ) to cover transportation charges for additional items.

    These (items) were required to replace defective
(items) which we received on our last order.

    We do not believe it is proper to pay transpor-
tation charges on additional materials needed to
replace defective product. Accordingly, we are
enclosing your invoice and request a full credit.

———————

REFUSAL
— Request To Publish

Dear (   ):

Thank you for forwarding your manuscript titled (   ).

Your manuscript has been reviewed by our editorial board. Unfortunately, they have decided that the manuscript does not meet our present publishing requirements.

We are hereby returning the manuscript and suggest that you forward it to other publishers.

Your interest is appreciated and we wish you every success.

———————

REFUSAL
— Request To Publish

Dear (   ):

    Thank you for your manuscript which we are herewith returning.

    (Company name) publishes only books in the field of (   ).

    We suggest that you send your manuscript to a publisher who specializes in your area of interest.

    We wish you every success.

———————

Dear (   ):

Thank you for sending us your order for (name of product).

(Name of Company) distributes our products through wholesalers who resell to dealers. Please contact one of the dealers in your area as listed on the enclosed sheet.

Anyone of these dealers will be able to supply your requirements.

Your order is being returned with this letter.

Your interest in our product is greatly appreciated.

REFUSAL
— Speaker

Dear (   ):

I wish to thank you for the invitation to speak at the (month) meeting of the (organization).

Unfortunately, I have a prior commitment and will be unable to address your group.

Perhaps you will consider me for another speaking date.

I certainly appreciate your interest.

———————

REFUSAL
— Unsolicited Ideas

Dear (   ):

    Thank you for your letter of (   ) suggesting ideas for (improving — inventing, etc.) our (product — publication, etc.).

    We are herewith returning your letter because (Company name) is not soliciting thoughts, ideas or suggestions regarding our (product line, etc.).

    While we appreciate your interest, we are requesting that you cease to submit ideas pertaining to our (manufacturing, marketing, publishing, etc.) activities.

    If consulting or other assistance is ever needed, we may consider the use of your services.

———————

REMINDER
— Appointment

Dear (   ):

This is a friendly reminder of your appointment scheduled for (hour) on (day, month, date, year).

Please be sure to bring with you any (x-rays, legal documents, etc.).

We are looking forward to your visit.

_____

RENT
— Notice of Increase

Dear (   ):

This is to notify you that your monthly rent will increase to ($) effective (date).

The increase is due to rising taxes and higher operating expenses.

We will continue to make every effort to control our costs while providing you with the high quality maintenance and services that you rightfully expect.

RENT
— Request for Payment, First

Dear (   ):

As of today, we have not received your rent payment for the month of (   ).

Under the terms of your lease, rent payments are due by the (date) of each month.

Perhaps you have overlooked this payment which is now past due.

Immediate payment of ($) is required.

RENT
— Request for Payment, Second

Dear (   ):

    With further regard to our letter of (   ), we have not received your rent for the month of (   ), which was due on the (   ).

    The procedure for delinquent rent is clearly stated in item no. (   ) of your lease.

    You are hereby notified that if payment of ($) is not received by (   ), and in accordance with the revised code of the state of (   ), we will instruct our attorney to initiate eviction proceedings.

———————

Dear (   ):

We are pleased to enclose a report of (subject) for (time period).

The in-depth report addresses the issue(s) of (   ). A complete examination is made of the various viewpoints of manufacturers, wholesalers, retailers and the government.

A synopsis with recommendations appears on page (   ).

We trust you will find the report to be informative and helpful. As always, we welcome your comments.

———

REPORT
— Year End

Dear (   ):

For the year ending (   ), we are pleased to report that (describe).

The year was marked by (describe). Significant highlights included (describe).

During the coming year, we plan to focus on (describe).

We look forward to (continued progress, etc.) in the months and years ahead.

———————

REPORTING A SUCCESS
— Project

Dear (   ):

Despite the many difficulties which I previously brought to your attention, I am happy to report that we have now found the right (distributor — hospital, etc.) in (state — county) and that an agreement has been successfully negotiated subject to your final approval.

We encountered many problems in the course of this search and I believe it would be useful to list them because they may be instructive in similar situations in the future:

1. (list problems)
2.
3.
4.

Nevertheless, we achieved our goal and I think the experience alone was well worth the time and effort. Of course, I am happy that we have established a firm basis for growth in the area.

I am looking forward to receiving your approval of the agreement and for the opportunity to personally review the situation with you.

———————

REQUEST
— Advance Payment

Dear (   ):

Thank you for your order no. (   ) for (   ).

It is our policy to request a (%) advance payment on initial orders from new accounts. If you will forward ($), we will ship your order immediately.

Once your initial order is paid and credit is established, we will place your firm on our normal net 30 payment terms.

Your interest in our product is greatly appreciated. We look forward to a long and mutually profitable relationship.

———————

REQUEST
— Appointment

Dear (   ):

We have just finalized our spring program which promises to be a big profit maker for your company.

I am anxious to review with you the key elements of the campaign. Accordingly, would you be available at your office on the morning of (day, month, date)?

Please contact me or my secretary and inform us of the time that would be best for you. If the date is not satisfactory, we will arrange a new time.

I am looking forward to sharing our exciting plans with you.

Dear (   ):

I wish to make an appointment with (   ) for the purpose of (describe).

I will be available on the dates of (   ), (   ) and (   ) with an early morning appointment preferred. If these dates are not satisfactory, other times may be arranged.

Please advise me of an appointment date.

Thank you.

REQUEST
— Better Seats

Dear (   ):

As a life member of the (   ) Alumni Club, I have had two season tickets for (   ) football games for more than 20 years. During this time, I have strongly supported the team at both home and away games.

I am writing to request an exchange for better seats between the 30 and 50 yard lines.

I will appreciate your giving this request every consideration and I look forward to hearing from you.

GO (   )!

———————

REQUEST
— Career Guidance Interview

Dear (   ):

Your friend, (name), has suggested that I contact you.

You may be aware that (organization) recently underwent a major restructuring. My position along with many similar positions was eliminated.

I am developing new career plans and believe that you, as a leader of the industry, would be able to give me some excellent advice.

I am not seeking a position with your company, but merely wish to receive your thoughts and guidance.

I will call you this coming Tuesday morning and hope that you will be willing to schedule a brief appointment.

———————

REQUEST
— Completion of
Performance Appraisals

Dear (   ):

The proper completion of performance appraisals is one of your most important responsibilities.

Enclosed are the annual performance appraisal forms for the employees under your supervision. Instructions for completing the evaluations and conducting interviews are enclosed with the forms.

We wish to emphasize the following:

1. Be honest.

2. Be objective and not subjective.

3. Substantiate all statements with factual information expressed in percentages or numbers wherever possible.

4. Reinforce the positive and encourage the employee to achieve greater career development.

5. Follow the check list of all factors that are to be considered.

Please return the confidential forms to my attention on or before (   ).

Dear (   ):

    I wish to express my appreciation for your recent purchase of (   ).

    May I ask for a favor? If you know of anyone who would benefit from this (product or service), I would appreciate your completing the enclosed card and returning it to me in the enclosed postage paid envelope.

    Thanks again and if I may be of any further assistance, please let me know.

———————

REQUEST
— Dividend Reinvestment Program

Dear (   ):

I recently purchased 100 shares of common stock in (Company name).

The certificate number (   ) is held in my name.

Please enter this stock in your automatic dividend reinvestment plan at the earliest opportunity. I would appreciate receiving a confirmation of this request.

Thank you.

_____

REQUEST
— Government Action

Dear (   ):

   I am writing to request your help in obtaining better service at the new (name of city) post office.

   Customer service at this new multimillion dollar facility continues to be deplorable. Postal patrons are often waiting in long lines because only one employee is working at the counter. Box mail is often not distributed until the middle of the morning which creates a problem for businesses such as ours. After a recent snow storm, the sidewalk to the main entrance had not even been cleared.

   Many residents of (name of city), drive to other communities in order to obtain proper service.

   I believe these views reflect the thoughts of many members of this growing community. Your efforts to improve service at the (name of city) facility would be greatly appreciated.

   I am looking forward to hearing from you.

———————

REQUEST
— Opinion

Dear (   ):

I wish to extend my heartiest congratulations on your graduation from (name of school, seminar or program). I know full well about the many hours of extra work the program requires while you are still carrying out your full-time responsibilities with (employer). I am sure that the (time) at (school) will enhance your movement up the ladder of success.

As a member of the Board of Trustees, we are continuously trying to keep the program as up-to-date as possible to enable it to meet the educational needs of (the school, field, community, etc.). I would like your assistance in appraising the (school, seminar, program, etc.). It doesn't have to be a formal paper or any thing of that kind, but it would be appreciated if you would just take the time to reflect on your experience and drop me a note regarding your impression.

You may want to consider, among other things, the curriculum, instructors and the overall value in terms of your career objectives. Your input will be used at future board meetings as we discuss plans for the school.

Once again, congratulations and the best of luck to you.

———————

REQUEST
— Permission To Use
Copyrighted Material

Dear (   ):

We are writing a college textbook on the subject of (   ). The title of the book will be (   ) and it will be published by (   ).

We have found your article on (   ) which appeared in the (   ) issue of (   ) to be of special interest. Your article clearly examines the subject of (   ) and offers many viewpoints for serious thought.

The specific paragraph of interest is as follows:

(Insert paragraph).

May we have your permission to include the above paragraph in our chapter on (   )? Of course, we will give you full credit and state that the paragraph was reprinted with permission. We will also be glad to provide you with a complimentary copy of the book when it becomes available.

We hope to hear favorably from you.

———————

REQUEST
— Post Employment Rejection Interview

Dear (   ):

Thank you for your letter of (date).

Naturally, I was disappointed that I was not selected for the position of (title). However, your consideration was greatly appreciated.

I am wondering whether you would be kind enough to give me some guidance as to how I might improve my resume and interviewing skills for future appointments.

I will call you next Tuesday and hope that you will give me some advice.

———————

REQUEST
— Preparation For Plant Tour

Dear (   ):

On (   ), a group of executives from (   )
will be visiting our Company. They are considering
our firm as a supplier.

A plant tour is scheduled for (   ). Naturally,
we wish to make a good impression on this
potentially large customer.

Please make every effort to ensure that our
factory is especially clean and conveys a very
productive and efficient manufacturing operation.

Thanks for your usual fine cooperation.

———————

REQUEST
— Product User Comments

Dear (   ):

    All of us at (Company) thank you for purchasing our product. Your (item) is designed to give you many years of dependable service.

This product was inspected by the following:

(individual)

    We encourage your comments.

Again, our sincere thanks.

(Company)

———————

REQUEST
— Recommendation For A Speaker

Dear (   ):

I need a favor.

As Program Chairman for the local (   ) Club, I am in charge of scheduling speakers for our luncheon meetings. We have a speaker opening during our meeting on (   ), at (time).

I know that you are very active in your country club and I thought you might be able to recommend a speaker who could talk about preparations for the upcoming national golf tournament.

I believe that our members would be interested in this vast undertaking.

Would you please look into this and let me know of any suggestions?

———————

REQUEST
— Reservation

Dear (   ):

I wish to reserve a room with a double bed for (days, month and dates).

I plan to arrive on (day) afternoon and will depart early on (day) morning.

Your forwarding a confirmation will be appreciated.

———————

Dear (   ):

It is with the deepest regret that I must submit my resignation from the (club) effective (date).

During the (no.) years of my membership, I have made many lasting friends and have enjoyed the fine activities and facilities of (club).

I must now say good-bye due to (relocation — retirement, etc.).

I have been very touched by my association and I will always hold a fondness in my heart for (club).

———————

RESIGNATION
— Employment

Dear (   ):

This is to inform you of my resignation from (employer) effective (date).

My decision is based largely on my plans to spend much of the year at my Florida home.

I have certainly enjoyed my many years of employment at (organization). The experience has been very rewarding.

You have my best wishes for continued success.

———————

RESIGNATION
— Employment

Dear (   ):

This is to notify you of my resignation from (employer) effective (date).

I am going to miss my many friends and wish to express my appreciation for (no.) years of valuable employment.

I will be glad to cooperate in any way to arrange for an orderly transfer of my responsibilities.

I extend best wishes to the (employer) for many years of continued success.

———————

RESUME
— Transmittal

Dear (   ):

 I am interested in a writing or editing position with your company. I am a free-lance writer with a wide range of experience.

 Enclosed are copies of business articles which I have written for a number of publications. I have also written chapters for college textbooks and business manuals.

 As an experienced writer, I believe that I could make a major contribution to your company. Enclosed is a complete resume.

 I would very much appreciate an interview to discuss my qualifications in greater detail. I look forward to your reply.

———————

Dear (   ):

I am a very industrious and enthusiastic person looking for a position with greater responsibility and challenge.

As you can see by the enclosed resume, my experience and qualifications make me an excellent candidate for the position of (title).

When I was in college at (name of college), I showed my management skills by (describe). During my (no.) years as an employee at (name of company), I was able to (describe). I am sure that I can achieve the same degree of success with your (organization).

I hope to hear favorably from you.

———————

RESUME
— Transmittal

Dear (   ):

    I am writing in response to the advertisement for a (position) which appeared in the (name of newspaper) on (date).

    I believe that my qualifications and experience closely parallel the requirements outlined in your ad. A complete resume is enclosed.

    I would welcome an opportunity to discuss my qualifications and career plans with you.

    Your contacting me would be greatly appreciated.

———————

Dear (   ):

    The position of (title) is the type of employment that I am seeking.

    After reviewing my enclosed resume, I am confident that you will agree that my qualifications match your requirements.

    I would appreciate an interview so that I may discuss my desire to work for your fine organization.

    I am looking forward to a timely and favorable reply.

———————

Dear (   ):

As the landscape season gets underway, you will certainly be hiring extra help for your crews. I have a good background of working with trees and shrubs. I enjoy physical labor while working outdoors. My qualifications would be assets to your firm.

As a part-time employee at (   ), I have learned business operations and know how to ensure customer satisfaction.

Enclosed is my resume. I would greatly appreciate an interview during my spring break which begins on (   ). I will call you next week to hopefully schedule an interview.

Thank you for your consideration.

_____

RESUME
— Transmittal

Dear (   ):

I wish to apply for the position of (title).

I am a graduate of (school) with a (name) degree majoring in (subject). A complete resume is enclosed.

I believe that my education, desire and enthusiasm would enable me to make an important contribution to your company.

Your granting me an interview so that I may personally review my qualifications and career plans would be greatly appreciated.

———————

Dear (   ):

I am seeking a more challenging career opportunity in (public relations — selling, etc.). Your employee, (name) has suggested that I contact you.

I am a graduate of (school) where I majored in (subject).

Since (year), I have been employed by a leading manufacturer of (product). As a (position), I have gained solid experience in (function). A complete resume is enclosed.

I believe that I could do an excellent job for your company.

Your providing me with an opportunity to personally review my qualifications would be greatly appreciated.

I look forward to hearing from you.

SALES
— Direct Mail Appeal

Dear (   ):

(Company name) is pleased to announce the availability of (product). The new product is the culmination of many years of scientific research.

The new (product) offers the following benefits.

1.

2.

3.

Users have already reported the following successes.

1.

2.

3.

The low cost of ($) will (strengthen your bottom-line — increase productivity, etc.).

Please call (phone no.) to receive additional information. *ACT TODAY!* Call *NOW!* It may be your best profit making decision of the year!

Dear (   ):

On behalf of the (School) Athletic Boosters Association, I hope we can count on you to again place an advertisement in this year's (school) football program book.

Your ad represents pride in our community and helps make our program possible. Enclosed are complete details.

We look forward to receiving your ad in support of the (nickname of team).

SOLICITATION
— General

Dear (　　　　):

Can you help?

The (organization) needs people like you to give time or money for (charity — campaign, etc.).

The (organization) (describe objective — benefits, etc.).

We hope you will participate actively. If you cannot, would you please send a contribution, no matter how small, to this fine and needy cause?

We hope to add your name to the many people who have already contributed.

———————

SOLICITATION
— Membership

Dear (   ):

For over (number) years, (organization) has actively supported the interests of its members.

(Organization) serves as a watchdog in Washington and makes its voice known on vital issues affecting your (business — hospital, etc.). Enclosed is a brochure describing the numerous services offered by (organization).

Your membership represents an investment that will pay many dividends. Membership fees are only ($).

Why not take a minute and send us a check today? It may be the best investment you ever made!

———————

SYMPATHY
— Death

Dear (   ):

    We were very saddened to hear of the passing away of (name).

    I wish to extend to you and to members of your family our deepest sympathy.

Dear (   ):

    This letter conveys our deepest sympathy on the loss of (name).

    Please know that (he/she) has a special place in our hearts. (First name) will be sorely missed.

Dear (   ):

I have just learned of your loss and extend my deepest sympathy.

At a time like this, words simply cannot express my feelings.

My prayers are with you.

Dear (   ):

The (company — school, etc.) wishes you to know how much (name) will be missed by (his/her) friends and associates.

(Name's) personality always radiated kindness and sincerity. We were all proud to call (name) a friend.

You have our deepest sympathy.

SYMPATHY
— Time of Need

Dear (   ):

Our prayers and thoughts are with you during this time of need.

All of us remember (name) as a happy and sincere friend.

Please take the comfort in knowing that you are not alone.

———————

TERMINATION
— Apartment Lease

Dear (   ):

This is to inform you that I will be vacating apartment no. (   ) on (day), (month), (year).

I understand that my security deposit of ($) will be refunded pending an inspection on the departure date.

I have enjoyed the apartment and will recommend it to others.

———————

WELCOME
— New Customer

Dear (   ):

    Thank you for choosing us to provide your
(   ).

    You may be assured that we will do our best to
earn your trust and confidence. We hope this is the
beginning of a long and mutually profitable relationship.

    If you have any questions, please feel free to call
me.

WELCOME
— New Employee

Dear (   ):

It is a real pleasure to welcome you to (organization).

The reputation of the (organization) is well known and your appointment is certainly in keeping with these high standards.

We look forward to working with you and extend our best wishes for every success.

Dear (   ):

We are so happy that you have decided to join our organization.

(Organization) has worked for (better schools — neighborhood improvements, etc.) since its beginning. You will definitely be a valuable addition to this fine group.

Welcome and good luck. Please feel free to call on me for any help you may need.

We look forward to your active participation in (organization).

WELCOME
— New Member

Dear (   ):

On behalf of our entire membership, I wish to extend a warm welcome to the (club — society, etc.).

We encourage you to become active in our organization and enjoy the many benefits of membership.

Enclosed is a booklet containing the history of the (club — society, etc.), a membership roster and a schedule of activities for the year.

I look forward to meeting you at the new members' luncheon scheduled to be held on (date) at (location). Additional information concerning the luncheon will be forthcoming.

Once again, welcome to the (club — society, etc.).

———————

WELCOME
— Promoted Employee

Dear (   ):

I was so happy to hear about your (appointment — promotion). It will be great working together.

Your expertise and willingness to try new approaches will make you a strong contributor to the success of our organization.

If I can be of any help to you, please feel free to call on me.

———————